The Hitcher.
Chris Coekin.

Intro: Camilla Brown
Design: Why Not Associates

Intro.
Camilla Brown.

Chris Coekin set out to make this body of work with a clear plan of action in mind and strict parameters for how he intended to do so. Since 2000 he has, on separate journeys, travelled around and across the United Kingdom from John o'Groats to Land's End, Liverpool to Dover, and Northern Ireland to Wales. His mode of transport was simple – hitchhiking, a choice that made him reliant on others and forced him to rescind a certain amount of control, being dependent on strangers to propel him on his way.

BECAUSE YOU WANTED A LIFT.

One element of the final work is a series of portraits Coekin took of the people who gave him a lift. They effectively selected themselves to become part of the work, through their split-second decision to give him a ride. This is interesting when one compares it to other journeys recorded by photographers who are part of the social documentary tradition, in which it is the photographer who decides whom and what to photograph. The subjects are usually unaware that they have become part of a body of work. Even those that are called 'concerned photographers', who live in amongst the people they photograph, remain in a voyeuristic perspective - outside of, and separate to, the subjects of the work. Coekin's project is by its very nature much more participative, and there is a different level of exchange between the photographer and those who are photographed. They all have the choice to take part, and invariably they are happy to oblige.

Coekin also chooses to place himself in the work, since another element is a series of self-portraits taken on self-timer with a small snapshot camera and processed by his local lab. In these, the artist becomes the actor in a self-constructed drama, playing The Hitcher. Interested in cinematic references, and numerous films that explore the latent macabre potential of a hiking

scenario, Coekin wanted part of the work to be about the underlying tension that surrounds the process of picking up an unknown man at the side of the road. In that sense, he is playing a part and we see his appearance change throughout the project. We see him frustrated, wet and cold, waiting in a lay-by, or carefree and relaxed in his summer shorts. We see his painful blistered and sunburnt feet - evidence of hardship and suffering for his art. This is what makes his work stand apart from so many others. We may get glimpses of Winogrand in shop window fronts or his shadow cast on the ground; more often, Friedlander will appear in his own images - but rarely is such a central core of a body of work the artist himself. This relates Coekin's practice more to performance art than to photography, with the artist as protagonist.

Another section of the work includes Coekin's photographs of the roadside detritus he comes across on his journeys. We see brightly coloured crisp packets and McDonald's cartons slung out of car windows and blown across intersections, landing in grass verges. We see discarded DVD players rendered obsolete and worthless so quickly by the pace of technological advancement. Coekin sees these objects as metaphors reflecting some of the negative aspects of contemporary British life. In some cases, though, these discarded objects take on a life and beauty of their own. We wonder why and how they got to where they are and what story lies behind them. In this respect, the work bears strong comparison to the British artist Keith Arnatt's witty and poetic observations of rubbish. Arnatt transforms the mundane into something more interesting and surreal through the process of photographing them.

Ultimately, this work is about a personal journey. As Mark Haworth-Booth was to comment on The English at Home, Bill Brandt's seminal body of photographs taken in 1930s Britain, "Brandt was one of a generation of young photographic explorers whose visas, it could be said, had already been issued by literature." Certainly, as mentioned in Coekin's text, he was influenced by both Jack Kerouac and Laurie Lee. As homage, Coekin visits Slad on his journey, the place that Lee was so keen to escape in his book As I Walked Out One Midsummer Morning. It is interesting to think that he was fleeing the very same 1930s England that Brandt had caught on film. Lee's travels to Spain, just at the outbreak of the Civil War, serve as a great example of a personal quest that gets bizarrely caught up in a significant moment of history. In retrospect, his insights into Spanish life and its people offer a fascinating record of a particular moment in time that quickly becomes a thing of the past.

It will be interesting to see how Coekin's work is read in the future. The fact that it exists at all stands as testimony to, and as a potential epitaph for, a way of travelling that seems set to disappear from our landscape in years to come. Certainly, over the time that Coekin was making this work, the number of hikers on our motorways diminished and more people seemed reluctant to pick him up. However, with ecological issues coming to the fore, car pooling and perhaps new versions of 'cyber'-hitchhikers might appear. It is hard to know what commentary this work might offer on the present, but there is no doubt that it is an important chapter in Coekin's practice.

For Kallum Rai

WHY DID YOU PICK ME UP?

LOOKED AS IF YOU HAD BEEN
WAITING FOR A WHILE AND
YOU WERE GOING TO NEWCASTLE
I SAW NO HARM IN IT.

You looked interesting - I like meeting people from other places.

cín a gooa

Single lad & I had space.
was in no rush to go anywhere.

A BIT OF COMPANY

THERE IS NO REASON

D.O.B	21 APRIL 1944
PLACE OF RESIDENCE	DRESTERNAN DERRYGONNELLY CO. FERMANAGH
OCCUPATION	ARCHITECT, PAINTER
START DESTINATION END DESTINATION	ENNISKILLEN OMAGH
REASON FOR JOURNEY	TO DISCUSS THE MANUFACTURE A STAINLESS STEEL SCULPTURE THE 10TH ANNIVERSARY MARKER MY. MOVING INTO MY NEW HO WITH STEEL FABRICATORS
DO YOU NORMALLY PICK UP HITCHHIKERS	NOT OFTEN
WHY DID YOU PICK ME UP	YOU LOOKED INTELLIGENT. I THOUGHT THE CONVERSATION MIGHT BE ENJOYABLE — I WAS RIGHT!
SIGNATURE	

KIND HEART

YOU WHERE GOING MY WAY
AND FOR THE COMPANY

ll pick up hikers
s I used to hike

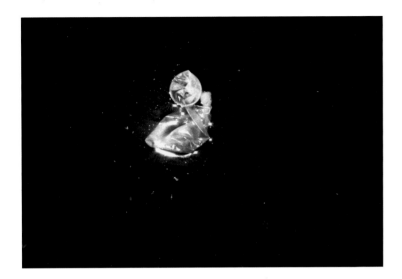

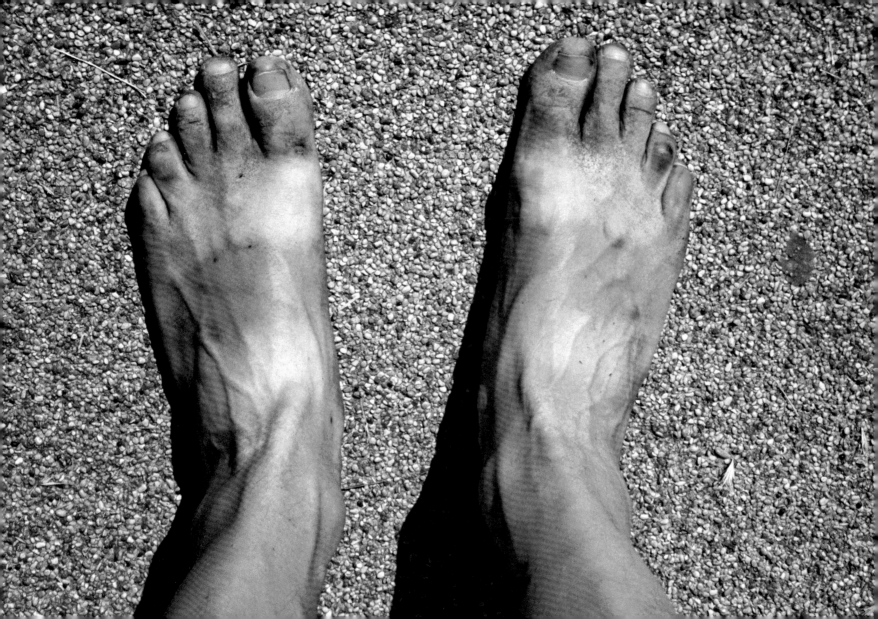

I suppose it all started, with Jack Kerouac's iconic Beat novel On The Road. I can't remember exactly how I stumbled upon it, but I think it was courtesy of an ex-girlfriend. Anyway, it left a pretty big impression on me and turned out to have a major impact on my life at a time when I had reached that place aptly referred to as the crossroads.

The job was dull, the beer was flat and the entertainment lousy. I couldn't see where my future lay. All I knew was that there had to be more to life than this job and its shackles. Jack and his boys were calling, the road trip appealed and I wanted to tread that sticky black Tarmacadam; I wanted to head into and off the horizon, recite poetry and strum Woody Guthrie; I wanted to jump a boxcar, ride in a Chevy and drop mescaline down in Mexico; I wanted to curl up under the stars and wake with a dark-skinned jasmine-fragranced beauty. In retrospect, of course, my dream of 'lighting out' like Kerouac was a self-conscious cliché, a romantic fantasy – but I felt I had been awakened.

That midsummer morning towards the back end of the 80s, I was awoken, awoken out of my dreams, by the sound of the 'dustbin men' dragging our rusty old bin down the alley. It was loud, one of those noises that gets right under your skin, eventually, as the week's waste – baked-bean tins, snap-crackle-and pop packets, potato peelings, beer cans and more – is spilled into the monster wagons. That was the day, the glorious day, when I was to set off on my travels. I'd been working, cash-in-hand, cleaning windows to earn a few bob for my journey. I recall that I had saved £230 – although, judging by my hangover, I'd probably spent a significant amount of it down the pub the previous evening.

There, on the Formica table in front of me, was the book that was to be my real inspiration: Laurie Lee's autobiographic As I Walked Out One

Midsummer Morning. It was cover side up, and it was this cover – of the 1988 Penguin edition – that provided the blueprint for my travel luggage. It consisted of a small green canvas bag and a tightly wrapped sleeping bag which I'd had since joining the Cub Scouts back in 1977. The sleeping bag had a musty stench to it – but hey, I was heading for the dust-drenched open road.

I sat at the front, on the top deck of the number 38 bus that was biding its time at the Monmouth Drive terminus on the Eyres Monsell Estate in Leicester. I was waiting for my travelling companion, another thrill-seeker who was disillusioned, a spiritual compatriot who longed to break free and chase down the sunset. Ian, aka the Big Fella, was going to join me. He bounded on to the bus and I could hear his panting and wheezing as he struggled up the stairs, dragging his luggage in his wake. He certainly hadn't gone for the minimalist option, and clearly didn't believe in travelling light like Laurie and myself. No, he had decided on the family-luggage-on-wheels option. 'Big Fella,' I exclaimed, 'we are about to set off for the open roads of Europe, and you have packed like we're going on a package holiday to Benidorm.'

I have to admit that, up to that point, the planning of our journey had mostly taken place after several Billy Ales. Although I was deadly serious about change, it dawned on me that the Big Fella probably wasn't as enthusiastic about shaking off the shackles as I was. Until our rendezvous on that 38 bus, I'd been led to believe he was quitting his 'boring' job in the tax office and heading off with me on a one-way ticket. It turned out that, just as I'd suspected, this was his two-week annual holiday, not his road to salvation.

After several memorable nights in Amsterdam (another story), we found ourselves at a service station next to an autobahn somewhere in southern Germany. Our intention – or at least mine – was to hitchhike our way through Europe. We were officially 'hitching virgins' and knew nothing about its etiquette or customs. On this particular day, on this particular spot, there seemed to be an unusually large number of hitchhikers, 'free spirits' who came in all shapes and sizes, both female and male. There were long-haired, shaven-headed, goatee-bearded, dreadlocked, pierced, tattooed and greater bearded types. Their clothing and decoration consisted of beads, bangles, big baggy trousers, Tibetan skull caps, reversed baseball caps, seashell necklaces, plenty of distressed denim and a faint whiff of petunia oil. Then there was the Big Fella: grey slacks, grey socks, sensible shoes, pin-striped shirt, pullover and grey suitcase on wheels. I, at least, had made an effort – or thought I had – with my Kerouac-inspired desert boots, Levis and T-shirt. And definitely, under no circumstances, had I considered wearing petunia oil!

The time had come for us to put ourselves at the mercy of 'The Road', to be guided by the compassion and benevolence of those good, good, drivers. 'OK then, start hitching,' said the Big Fella.

'You do it,' I said. 'No, it was your idea,' he yelled. 'No, go on, you start,' I replied. 'It's your fucking big idea, now stick out your thumb or I'm off,' barked the Big Fella. It can't have been a pretty sight – two grown men, one 6ft tall the other 6ft 5in and weighing 16 stone, squabbling at the roadside somewhere in Bavaria. The seasoned hitchhikers looked on with some amusement at our shenanigans, observing our heated debate as we waved our fists at each other and threw around verbal insults.

Eventually, I stepped up to the breach. Hesitantly, and with caution, I stuck out my thumb. Christ, it felt weird, like nothing I'd ever done before. My thumb felt like it was on fire and was glowing like a Belisha beacon. Who would have thought that such a simple act as holding out a thumb would stir such emotions? I felt nervous as the adrenalin started to flow through my awkward body. I felt uncomfortable, exposed and vulnerable. I felt that, somehow, I was offering myself up for some pagan ritual. I felt soulless, like a mannequin – and indeed, I was now in the shop window and on offer. It occurred to me that any potential lift-giver would have very little time, probably only a matter of seconds, to make a decision about my character. Such a judgment could only be based on my external appearance and the driver's preconceptions about it. This disturbed me, adding to my woes. I began to consider my stance and my facial expression. Maybe I should smile more, maybe I shouldn't slouch, maybe I should play hard to get.. fuck, this was getting

complicated. Perhaps I should simply strap a big sign around my neck – 'Please give me a lift. I am a good person of good character (can provide references), with excellent manners and a strong bladder.' Good God, what had I let myself in for? What sort of maniac would stop? It was bound to be some nutter who would rob me at knife point. It occurred to me that my next journey could be my last – bound, gagged, locked in a car boot and never heard of again. I began to think I had made a big mistake, that maybe this hitchhiking malarkey wasn't such a good idea. Perhaps the Big Fella had the right idea, that a two-week holiday and a pragmatic return to the day job was the only way forward.

I glanced over at him, perched on his ludicrous big grey suitcase, legs crossed, giggling like a naughty schoolboy at my feeble attempts to attract a lift. 'Fuck you and your case,' I yelled, sticking out my thumb with renewed vigour and real conviction. Several cars slowed down and their drivers appeared to take an interest. On one occasion, I ran after a decelerating vehicle but, as I approached, received a volley of insults and 'the finger' from its young occupants. I figured that hitchhiking was a bit like fishing: you optimistically cast your hook and then bide your time, occasionally getting a nibble, panicking a bit and striking too soon, only for the fish to swim off.

Then it happened. A car – I can't recall the make or model, but it was big, black and German – took the bait. It came to a halt further up the road, with the rays of the midday sun bouncing off its frosted black windows. The Big Fella stopped giggling, his amused expression was replaced by one of nervous anticipation. He looked over at me and I froze, suspended in time, still holding out my thumb, unsure what to do next. I'd really gone and done it now. The driver blasted his horn and the car waited motionless, 20 yards ahead, its engine ticking over. I looked over my shoulder and saw that some of our fellow hitchhikers had started making their way over to the shiny black chariot. That was our lift, it was my catch, and nobody was going to steal it. It was my destiny, I believed. I motioned over to the Big Fella to get a move on and he caught up with me, dragging his case like a bag of swag in the dirty grey rubble. We soon reached the strange vehicle with its anonymous driver, well ahead of our rivals. We stood on opposite sides of the car, the Big Fella beside the front passenger window, I beside the driver's. The car's misty black windows slowly opened to the accompaniment of a faint electrical buzzing. We could now eyeball our mystery Good Samaritan and potential travelling companion. Simultaneously, with mouths agape, like something out of a Laurel and Hardy film, we peered at each other in disbelief over the car roof. Again we stooped down and looked inside, again our eyes met in horror. Then, in almost perfect unison, we spluttered, 'Fuck, he's got no arms!'

The driver, a middle aged man, addressed us in German — a slight problem, since neither I nor the Big Fella spoke a word of the language.

'Do you speak English?' I asked. 'Of course I do, where are you going?' the driver replied. It occurred to us that we hadn't thought about such inconsequential details as our destination. 'North?' the Big Fella suggested. 'OK, get in,' said the driver, with noted enthusiasm. Nervously we clambered into the car, clunked and clicked our seatbelts and contemplated our immediate future. The armless driver was controlling the car entirely with his feet, using some contraption adapted from the steering column and pedals. He was in the mood for conversation and often looked me straight in the eye — a little disconcerting, since I was sitting in the rear passenger seat. Our new friend was a good conversationalist, intelligent and witty, and the Big Fella and I began to relax and enjoy the journey in the company of this genuine and honest person. We watched in amazement at his driving agility, made more remarkable by the fact that we were going very, very fast along the autobahn. Before we knew it, we had reached the end of the road — yet the journey was only just beginning.

Chris Cookin
May 07.

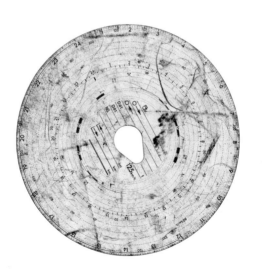

 LOOKED NORMAL

ALWAYS PICKUP HITCHHIKERS AND
YOU DIDN'T LOOK TOO SMELLY.

NOT AS A RULE
TO ROB YOU.

FERT SORRY. 1.

Nice day, good mood and
You looked hot + bothered

Someone to ta[l]
on the Jou[r]

Hull is a hard place to leave.
Elisa knows from experience &
has hitched from the same site.

LOOKED LIKE You
NEEDED A LIFT IN MORE THAN
ONE WAY.

Acknowledgments

First and foremost to all the good people
who stopped to give me a lift over the years
and participated in the work, thank you for
your generosity and kindness.

Special thanks to Andy Altmann for his
enthusiasm and fantastic design. Camilla
Brown for her belief and encouragement.
Chris Grawe, Jeff and Fred Keene for helping
me out once again... much appreciated. Andrew
Purvis, Joe Morse and young Mark. Fulvio
Porcellini, Dewi Lewis. University College
for the Creative Arts, The Photographers'
Gallery. Finally, lots of love to my parents,
Beckie and Kallum Rai x

Also by Chris Coekin
Knock Three Times
Published by Dewi Lewis Publishing
ISBN: 1 904587 28 3